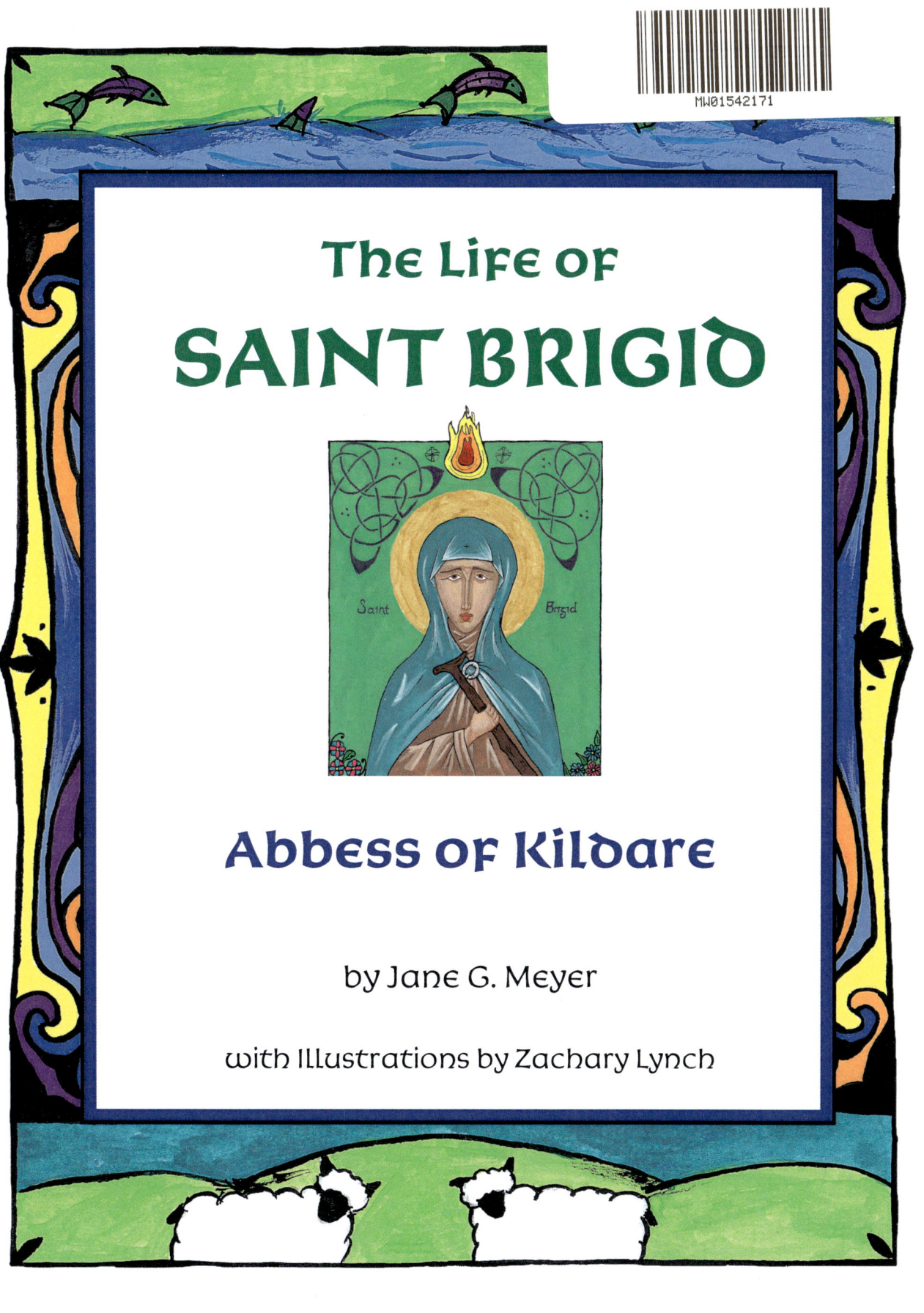

The Life of
SAINT BRIGID

Abbess of Kildare

by Jane G. Meyer

with Illustrations by Zachary Lynch

THE LIFE OF ST. BRIGID
ABBESS OF KILDARE

Text copyright © 2009 by Jane G. Meyer
Illustrations copyright © 2009 by Zachary Lynch

Originally published by Ancient Faith Publishing, PO Box 748, Chesterton Indiana, 46304 (formerly known as Conciliar Press)

Second printing © 2017 by Jane G. Meyer
Illustrations copyright © 2017 by Zachary Lynch

Printed in the United States

All rights reserved. No part of this publication may be reproduced by any means, electronic, mechanical, photocopying, recording, scanning, or otherwise, without the prior written permission of the author and illustrator.

ISBN : ISBN-13: 978-1976432590
ISBN-10: 1976432596

To my Madeleine,

whose heart breaks for the homeless.

With the help of St. Brigid, may this

tenderness and compassion continue

to reign in your heart.

—J.G.M.

To my family:

the faithful at Archangel Michael's

in Pueblo, Colorado.

—Z.L.

In ancient days a little girl was born.

Her father was an Irish chieftain,
but her mother was a slave,
a Christian slave who worked
in the chieftain's house.
When the chieftain found out
a child was to be born and
heard the prophecies about her—
that one day she would have a
mighty influence over Ireland—
he sold the mother.
"But when the child is grown,"
the chieftain said,
"return her to my house!"

Brigid was a fair and lively child, born in the humble house where her mother cooked and cleaned and tended many beasts.

Brigid learned these ways as she grew, and learned the ways of a Christian, too, to pray and sing and speak of love and gladden those around her.

As a young girl, her devotion to the triune God grew strong. Nothing in Brigid's life was too small for Christ's attention. She even sang to her pantry,

> "O God, bless my pantry!
>
> Pantry which the Lord has blessed.
>
> Mary's Son, my friend,
>
> come and bless my pantry!"

And God blessed her pantry so much that milk and butter overflowed the jugs and vats that tried to hold them in.

But once she was grown, the time came for Brigid to return to the house of her father, lord of the lands of Faughart. A beautiful countryside it was, with rolling hills and streams that glittered down the slopes and sheep that baaed their days away, munching on the sweet grass.

There Brigid was given charge of her father's kitchens and dairy. But it did not take long for the chieftain to realize that bringing Brigid into his home would create troubles he had never imagined.

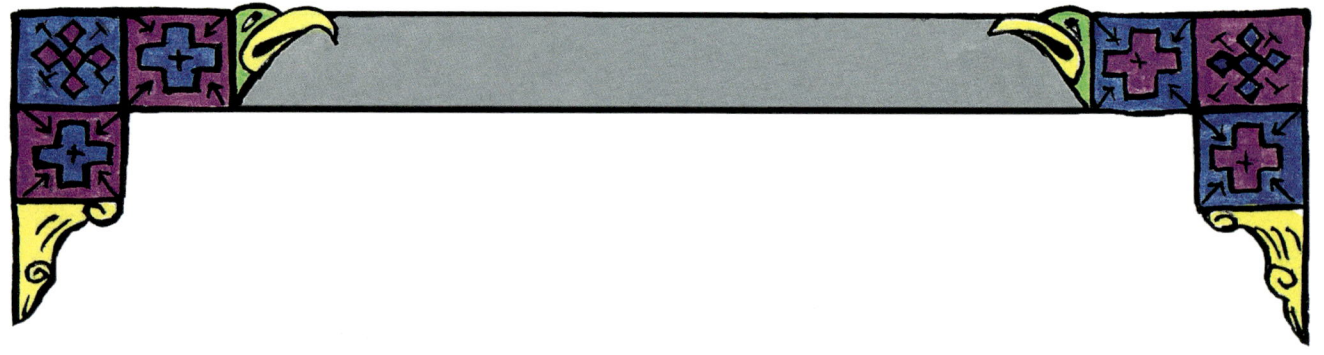

Brigid saw Christ in everyone she met, and had a particular love for those less fortunate than herself.

When the poor came knocking at the kitchen doors,

    Brigid handed out loaves of bread,

    jars of butter and jugs of milk.

    With her heart and hands opened wide,

    she even gave away the food

    meant for the chieftain himself!

Finally, the chieftain had had enough of Brigid's generosity with his beloved things. So he bundled her into his chariot and rode off to sell her to a neighboring king.

While Brigid waited in the chariot for him to settle his business, an unfortunate leper approached her for alms. Brigid searched the chariot for food or coin, but found nothing to give the poor beggar. Until her eyes alighted on her father's warrior sword, the sign of who he was, the symbol of his strength and rule. The sword leaned against the inside of the chariot door, glimmering in the sunlight.

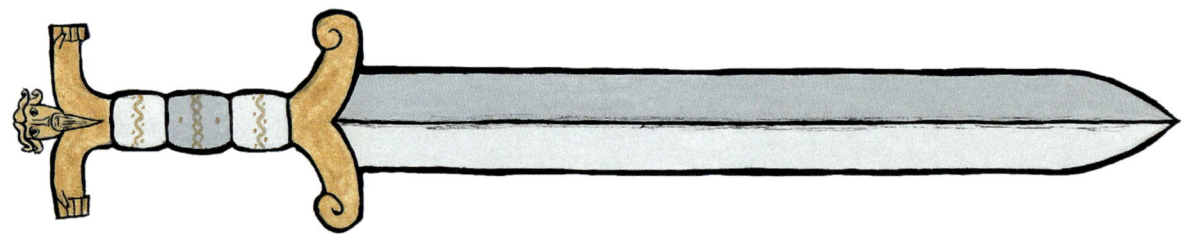

When her father returned and found his sword gone, he grumbled and growled and shook his fists, then presented young Brigid to the king.

The king was wise and asked the girl, "You take your father's wealth and distribute it. How much more would you take mine, seeing I am nothing to you, and give all I own away?"

Brigid of course replied that she would indeed give all the king's wealth away, if she only had the chance!

The king counseled the chieftain to release Brigid from slavery and make her a free woman. He then gave Brigid's father a sword to console him for his loss, and bade him take the girl away.

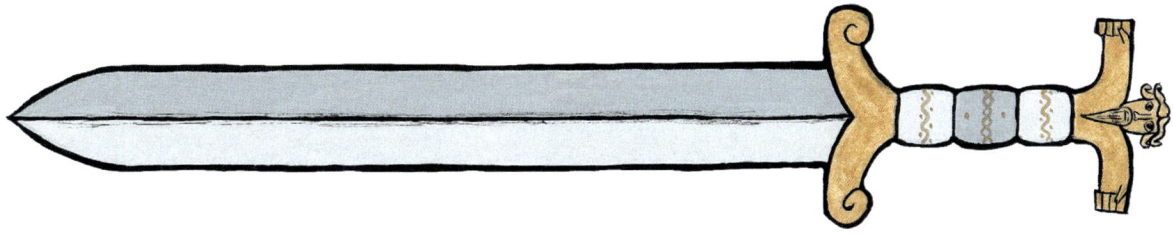

The chieftain, still smarting from Brigid's treatment of his things, came up with yet another plan to tame and teach his daughter. He freed her, as the king had asked, and found a suitor for her to marry.

When Brigid refused to marry the chosen man, a gentle and handsome poet, her family was furious. She had long desired a life devoted purely to Christ, with no tie to husband or home. When they pressed her yet again, Brigid scarred her own fair and youthful face. Her family finally understood and yielded to her wish and will.

Brigid's dreams grew grand, and knowing how faithful God had always been, she didn't hesitate to embark on something new. So she took the veil and became a nun, marrying Christ and His Church instead of man. And as a sign of God's hand upon her, the scar on her cheek was healed as the priest placed the white veil upon her head.

Along with seven other women, Sister Brigid approached the king, the same king who so wisely refused to buy her, and petitioned him for land to build a monastery. When he refused, she asked if she could have only so much land as her humble cloak could cover.

The king agreed, and Brigid laid down her cloak. But he was shocked when her cloak began to spread—from beside her feet, across an expanse of fertile land, until it covered the rolling green Curragh itself. So this is where Brigid became Abbess of Kildare, planting the cornerstones of her church near a high and beloved oak tree.

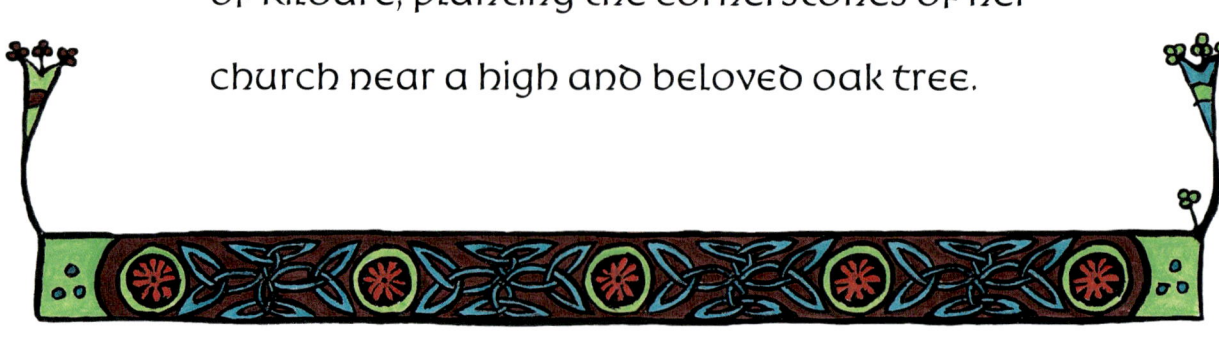

Brigid became an abbess, but she was a shepherdess, too. Not only did she tend her sheep on the rolling green hills, but she continued to tend the poor, giving freely from her stores and pantry as she had always done. And her community grew in numbers, until both monks and nuns lived under the abbess's care in Kildare, until thousands filled the place, offering joyous praise to the Holy Trinity.

But one convent could not contain all of the Irish women who wanted to follow Brigid's example. So she prayed for abundance again and again, and Christ favored each request. Brigid founded countless communities of nuns, until the convents reached from sea to sea across the green expanse of Ireland.

To care for all these women and the people both pagan and Christian that she loved, Brigid traveled often. She suffered accidents and cold, worked miracles of healing and visited kings. On one of her journeys she comforted an old pagan chieftain as he lay dying.

She found the chieftain in a desperate state, raving so that even the servants feared him. As Brigid sat by his bed, silently braiding the rushes that covered the floor, he became calm and asked, "What are you making?"

"This is a cross," the abbess said, "which I make in honor of the Virgin's Son, who died for us upon a cross of wood."

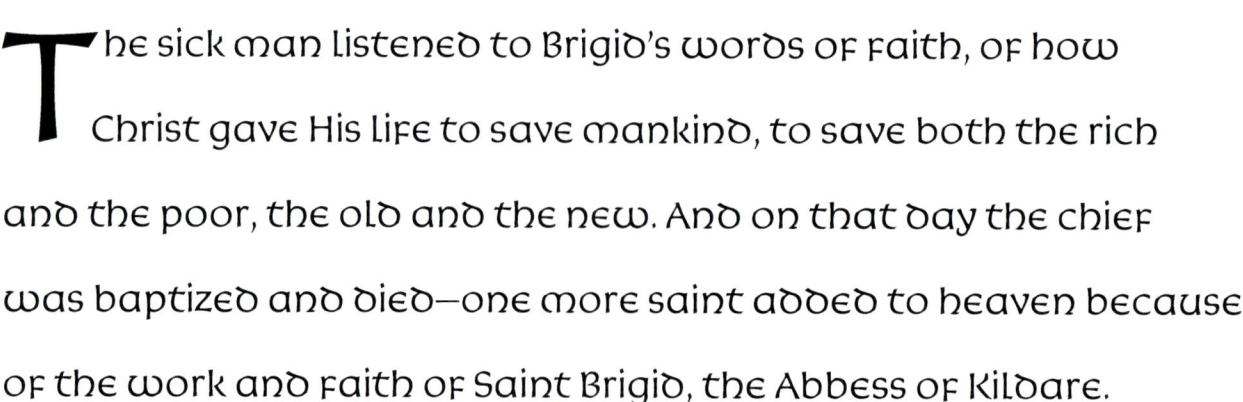

The sick man listened to Brigid's words of faith, of how Christ gave His life to save mankind, to save both the rich and the poor, the old and the new. And on that day the chief was baptized and died—one more saint added to heaven because of the work and faith of Saint Brigid, the Abbess of Kildare.

Saint Brigid lived a long life full of deeds dedicated to Christ. She is still known today for her generous and joyous spirit and her determination to spread the word of Christ's love; as a patron of travelers, healers, and midwives, and protector of flocks and herds and newborn babies. She died on the first of February in the year 525. And through her prayers she blesses our pantries still, as we cook and clean for those we know, and for those needy strangers who pass our door.

Irish Rune of Hospitality

I saw a stranger yestreen;

I put food in the eating place,

drink in the drinking place,

music in the listening place,

and in the name of the Triune

he blessed myself and my house,

my cattle and my dear ones, and the lark said in her song

often, often, often,

goes the Christ in the stranger's guise,

often, often, often,

goes the Christ in the stranger's guise.

May we follow Saint Brigid's example and receive the Christ in the stranger's guise. Saint Brigid, pray to God for us.

Kontakion of Saint Brigid *(Tone 4)*

The holy virgin Brigid full of divine wisdom,
went with joy along the way of evangelical childhood,
and with the grace of God
attained in this way the summit of virtue.
Wherefore she now bestows blessings
upon those who come to her with faith.
O holy Virgin, intercede with Christ our God
that He may have mercy on our souls.

About the Author and Illustrator:

Jane G Meyer is a children's book author and editor who lives in Santa Barbara, California, with her husband and three children. She's an admirer of the Gaelic language and Irish culture, and after studying the life of Saint Brigid and visiting the land Brigid helped change, she wanted to share her love of the saint with children. She hopes others will be inspired to love and give to their neighbor as Saint Brigid did.

Born in Colorado, Zachary Lynch developed a strong attraction to Celtic spirituality, in particular to Saint Patrick, while exploring his Irish heritage. As a young man, his devotion to Irish saints grew as he dabbled in Irish poetry and Celtic artwork. Eventually he began his own quest for the Christianity that Saint Patrick and Saint Brigid brought to Ireland, and found his spiritual home in the Orthodox Church. Since then he has been ordained to the priesthood and lives in Colorado with his wife, Natalia, and their five children.

Made in the USA
Monee, IL
17 February 2025

12435871R00021